*I*nspired
into
*I*nspiration

Brett A. Martinez

ISBN 978-1-63844-137-3 (hardcover)
ISBN 978-1-63844-138-0 (digital)

Christian Faith Publishing, Inc.
832 Park Avenue
Meadville, PA 16335
www.christianfaithpublishing.com

Printed in the United States of America

If I Can Dream

In dedication to all the people
who have given me the
inspiration to dream.
Brett A. Martinez

Inspired into Inspiration

When you inspire somebody, you lift
them up from where they're at. And
then when it turns into inspiration, you
not only lift that person up from where
they're at, but they are able to maintain
that lift, for it is no longer in words but
in their hearts.

God is faith, and faith is his word to us. For without faith we are nothing, but what the world is, so we must rise above the worlds abilities and rise to his ability to finish where Jesus, his Son, has left off for us to continue the work he set in him.

Therefore, the Bible is more than just a book, the living manual of God's will. The instructions to live in grace to serve God's purpose.

*B*elieving
*I*nto
*B*eyond
*L*iving
*E*vidence

We sleep, we dream, and then we awake
to fulfill the promise of God's eternal sake.
Joel 2:28 NKJV: And it shall come to pass afterward
that I will pour out My Spirit on all flesh;
your sons and your daughters shall
prophesy,
your old men shall dream dreams,
your young men shall see visions

Hand in Hand

There was a time and on this earth,
A Child was born in heaven's birth.
Coming to save and not destroy,
What all can see in praise and joy.
To shape and mold the imaged life,
To make and mend erasing strife.
For He will lift when shattered down,
And raise us to His Holy Crown.
Hand in hand we walk as one,
Just like the Father had
walked His Son.

Why complain about the mile
when we can help complete
a smile.

Day by Day

Day by day we walk through wrath,
We see how far, we walk the path.
To the point where we must be,
Within the heart where faith will see.
There is no limit, there is no end,
From the laughs we share,
to the hearts we mend.
For the sun may rise to
an early dawn,
And the night will come
when the day is gone.
Up we get and down we lay,
For the gift we hold
is in what we pray...
Day by day

A child soon grows up
when things are let go
and left behind.

My Prayer

Now I lay me down to sleep,
With this dream I hold to keep.
With a world so bright and clear,
Where there are no doubts,
there is no fear.
And the enemy you had
is now a friend,
There are no whispers,
there is no pretend.
For all the happiness
and no despair,
Is from all the loving
and all the care.
So as I kneel and as I pray,
Let there be another
dawn for another day.

To dream with him
is to trust his love.

"For God so loved the world that He gave
His only begotten Son, that whoever
believes in Him should not perish but have
everlasting life" (John 3:16 NKJV).

My Friend

The hand is there to take and hold,
To bring to heart the bitter cold.
To comfort those who are dismayed,
And warm the soul to never fade,
The ship is wrecked though
we may think,
Above He stands and not to sink.
A cry may come and
the tear will fall,
Who wipes the water, wipes it all.
We praise the Lord for
the gift He gave.
The path we follow,
in Him we crave.

Dreams should never
be shattered,
but put together
brick by brick.

"A time to kill, And
a time to heal;
A time to break down,
And a time to build up;"
(Ecclesiastes 3:3 NKJV).

14

Wings of Love

Love is in the heart no
matter where we look,
The hand wipes the tear in
the opening of His book.
So tender is the word and
so gentle is His touch,
To set us at an ease with
the love He shows so much.
Like the calmness of the waters
and the stillness of the trees,
With the coolness of the air
as He blows into the breeze.
On the heights of His heaven
and in the mysteries far above,
Higher than the skies
we soar on wings of love.

When love is
thought to be lost,
just remember
who paid the cost.

"When Jesus therefore had
received the vinegar, he said, 'It
is finished,' and he bowed his
head, and gave up the ghost."
(John 19:30 KJV)

Step-by-Step

Step-by-step is the instruction to His book,
From the turning of the pages, to
the Word in which we look.
We meditate we ponder and when
we hear His voice,
The word in which we choose is
the vision of our choice.
And when the truth is within us,
then the trust is our deed,
We stand for what is right, in
this He guaranteed.
No man shall come against us, no
weapon shall be used,
He took our pains and sorrows, with
stripes for all was bruised.
We praise, we pray, and then we pursue,
For the hope He sees is the faith in you.

Hope is the future
of what faith
holds today.

"Now faith is the substance of things hoped
for, the evidence of things not seen"
(Hebrews 11:1 NKJV).

Follow That Dream

Follow your instincts, follow your Guide,
Follow that dream deep down inside.
Never turn back and never let go,
Make that dream come true
and let it show.
For it doesn't have to be done
on any special day,
Anytime of the year is alright, okay.
So do it now and don't let yourself wait,
Do it this moment, this minute
and don't hesitate.
Follow that dream and you may lead,
To anything you want,
to the love you need.

Life is a thin line,
our faith depends on
how we thread it.

"Those who sow in
tears Shall reap in joy"
(Psalm 126:5 NKJV).

The Beginning

I love to write so now I say,
There will be what has come a day.
When down from heaven
right on to earth,
He gave His life to renew our birth.
Like a child is loved and love is He,
God stretched His hand to set us free.
The word is life to what is said,
We fulfill the trust by our daily bread.
To love is to heal that which is lost,
God has delivered for His
sake was the cost.

Truth opens the gate to what was once shut by a lie.

"Jesus said to him, 'I am the way, the truth, and the life. No one comes to the Father except through Me'" (John 14:6 NKJV).

A Touch

Like a flower gets a sprinkle
and the land needs the rain,
With His touch upon the earth
in victory we gain.
A seed to which we started
in life we will abound,
In all of God's creation through
Jesus we have found.
To blossom up so gently
by the waters of His touch,
Without the understanding, though
with love He shows so much.
On earth is all in heaven, just
look at what you see,
The gift is in the heart, to whom
is taken from the tree.
And forever is the hand He holds,
In a touch, The Living Book
he never folds.

If we give God our time,
he'll give us eternity.

Every change has
it's beauty,
upon the wings
that set us free.

"Therefore, if anyone is
in Christ, he is a
new creation; old things
have passed away; behold, all
things have become new"
(2 Corinthians 5:17 NKJV).

Folding hands are the hands
that unfold to God's heart.

"Therefore humble yourselves under
the mighty hand of God, that He
may exalt you in due time, casting
all your cares upon Him, for
He cares for you."
(1 Peter 5:6–7 NKJV)

$\mathcal{L}ove$

When you say love, you're ready to start,
A brand-new beginning with your heart.
Not in pieces but as a whole,
To promise your heart along
with your soul.
To be beside her when times get bad,
To hold her so gently
when she's so sad.
Some say love is like a river,
For the water is all the
love you can give her.
And some say love is like a flower,
For it blossoms so beautifully
after every shower.

Sometimes we have to let things shatter in order to pick up his peace.

"Peace I leave with you, My peace I give unto you" (John 14:27 KJV).

The Life
of a Seed

The life of a seed
is to plant it,
To nurture it and
let it grow.
To plant it, we put
it in good soil.
To nurture it, we
don't let the weeds
of influence grow
around it.
And to let it grow,
We trust in God to
what we sow.

What can be drawn from heaven
can be painted here on earth.

Label for Love

Life is so delicate,
So handle with care,
In order not to let love shatter.
Must be put through a
gentle cycle,
Never to shrink.
Iron regularly to keep out the
spots, wrinkles and blemishes.
And when necessary,
Hand wash the tender moments
that deposit straight to
the heart.
CAUTION
Never remove the Hand that
we all hold that helps us
through the wear and tear,
which becomes neatly folded
in His unconditional love,
That everlasting care.

Life is uncertain,
but eternity is sure.

"So we fix our eyes not on what is seen, but
on what is unseen. Since what is seen
is temporary, but what is unseen is eternal"
(2 Corinthians 4:18 NIV).

To see is that what comes and
goes, though the eyes are true
to what comes and grows.

Once Upon a Dream

Once upon a dream at a far, far reach,
Was a land of promises and hopes that teach.
To never give up and always stand tall,
To always take pride and never to fall.
To help one another in what they may need,
To inspire the weak and straighten the deed.
For a dream is not a dream until you
learn to let go of the fear,
That is holding the dream from coming near.
Dreams are so difficult, so difficult to be,
For I dream the impossible I have
yet and hope to see.

Changed to be changed.
Every day should remind us
that every day is brand-new.

Sometimes books don't show
what life holds in trust.

Do not fear change,
for it is one beauty
coming upon
another.

Love is such a distant word
until we choose to make
it unconditional.

"Draw near to God and He
will draw near to you"
(James 4:8a NKJV).

Faith is...
When we reach out
to the invisible
to draw from the
impossible.

"Now faith is the substance of
things hoped for, the evidence
of things not seen."
(Hebrews 11:1 NKJV)

Faith—Someone who believes in more than what they can see.

Feelings can be interrupted,
but faith can be trusted.

"For we walk by faith,
not by sight"
(2 Corinthians 5:7 NKJV).

The more we trust in God,
the more we'll follow
his word.

42

Love gives the
opportunity
to let go,
and to pick
up what
love offers
to grow.

"And now abide faith, hope,
love, these three;
But the greatest of these *is* love"
(1 Corinthians 13:13 NKJV).

The greatest gift is
when we give it away.

Words are made to follow
just as the Word is
made to guide.

Love is...
When joy
touches you
instead of hurt.

"My brethren, count it all joy
when you fall into various trials,
knowing that the testing of
your faith produces patience"
(James 1:2–3 NKJV).

Every day is brand-new.
So live it, and don't let
the day grow old.

The more you get into him,
the more you get out
of yourselves.

And planted in the
beauty grows,
From a helpless bud to
His promised rose.

"Being confident of this very
thing, that He who has begun a
good work in you will complete
it until the day of Jesus Christ"
(Philippians 1:6 NKJV).

You don't have to have
the intelligence to do it,

just the heart to fulfill it.

"Then the angel said to her, 'Do not be
Afraid, Mary, for you have
found favor with God.'"
(Luke 1:30 NKJV)

When we ask,
don't expect our own way.
But receive in God's best.

When we can't see from
the valley below,
it is on top of the mountain
where our praise will show.

Submission

(A submitting, or
surrendering, obedience.
to yield to the control
or power of another.)
To submit and yield to the
presence of God.
To pray for those
who fight,
And fight for those
who believe.

"Oh death, where is your victory?
Oh death, where is your sting?"
(1 Corinthians 15:55 AMPC).

Don't let the problem dwell on you,
just let the promise shine through.

No matter how long it takes,
his patience lasts a lifetime.

There is always a but
when we are in a rut.
But there always is a plan
when we rest in his hand.

The trust is in the truth
of shaping and molding the times.

"Therefore submit to God.
Resist the devil and he will flee
from you. Draw near to God
and He will draw near to you"
(James 4:7–8a NKJV).

When we read God's Word,
we don't waste time.
For his Word adds steps
to the mountain we will climb.

Poetry is an art.
Only the heart can understand.

"Blessed are the pure in
heart, For they shall see God"
(Matthew 5:8 NKJV).

In Him,
change our thinking,
And start thanking.

"This is the day the Lord has made;
We will rejoice and be glad in it"
(Psalm 118:24 NKJV).

What is more precious than life itself
is helping others live it.

Dreams are planted
so miracles can grow.

Time
The distance
between
us and obedience.

"Immediately the Spirit drove Him
into the wilderness"
(Mark 1:12 NKJV).

In God's Word
The more depth we root,
Is the more truth we draw.

Trials...

Satan wants to make
us weaker with them,
But God wants to make
us stronger in him.

"For Christ sake. For
when I am weak, I am strong"
(2 Corinthians 12:10 NKJV).

God is always good
at making nothing
into something.

Nothing is more beautiful
than having a heart to his whisper.

The Walk

Keep to the right,
And don't let the wrong
trip you.

Seasons come and seasons go,
Seasons change so love can grow.

"To everything there is a season"
(Ecclesiastes 3:1a NKJV).

Being a child of God,
we not only grow up with Jesus,
we are made to blossom in him.

Volunteering is...
In sharing with no
strings attached,
only the love that
is in the patch.

I Believe...

What is it that you believe?
For what you believe on the outside
can be different from what you
believe on the inside.
On the outside you try with a must,
on the inside you rely on a trust.
For out here what you believe
comes and goes,
but what is in here just builds
as it grows.

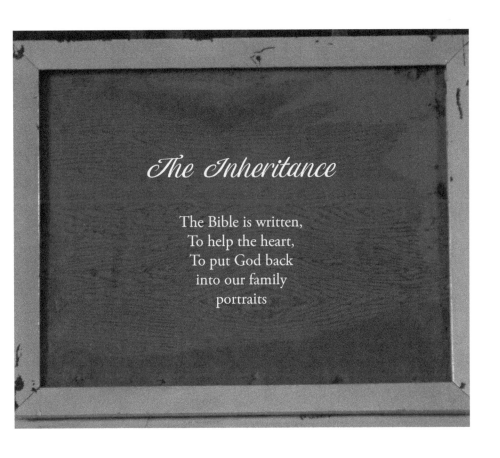

The Inheritance

The Bible is written,
To help the heart,
To put God back
into our family
portraits

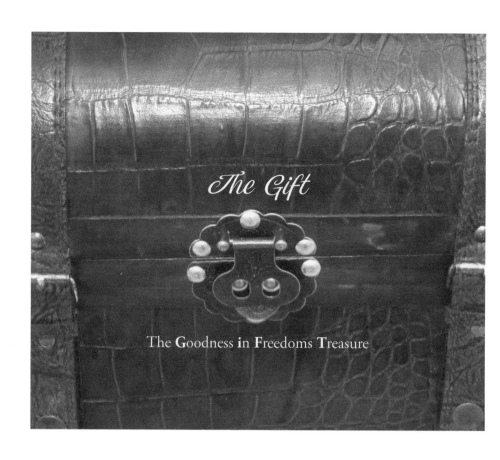

The Gift

The **Goodness** in **Freedoms** **Treasure**

Home Run
Letting our flaws play
in his favor

"Therefore I take pleasure in infirmities,
in reproaches, in needs, in persecutions,
in distresses, for Christ's sake. For when
I am weak, then I am strong"
(2 Corinthians 12:10 NKJV).

The Bible is our ladder
to help us climb to what
is out of reach.

"Then he dreamed, and behold
a ladder was set up on the earth,
and its top reached to heaven;
and there the angels of God were
ascending and descending on it"
(Genesis 28:12 NKJV).

In Him,
truth fulfills
what trust plows and tills.

Let yesterday go,
Take hold of today,
And let our faith rest
in tomorrow.

Pictures are to remind us
of where we've been,
and should encourage us
to keep going forward.

Encouragement to the heart
is like what teamwork
is in a task.
Encouragement
When all the we's work together
to help unfold the precious you

"that their hearts may be encouraged, being knit together in love,
and attaining to all riches of the full assurance of understanding,
to the knowledge of the mystery of God,
both of the Father and of Christ"
(Colossians 2:2 NKJV).

A smile is like a bowl of
sweetness,
that is ready to give
out to every frown.

In Him,
we are never defeated.
Only the walk is needed.

Let faith lead the way,
so our feelings can
enjoy its display.

"For we walk by faith, not by sight"
(2 Corinthians 5:7 NKJV).

Don't be all talk.
Let walk have its turn.

GOD
Goodness Offered Daily

"Oh, taste and see that the LORD is good" (Psalm 34:8 NKJV)

Piece to Peace
To every piece we let go,
God gives us the peace to
help us grow.

"Peace I leave with you, My peace I give you;
not as the world gives do I
give to you. Let not
your heart be troubled, neither let it
be afraid." (John 14:27 NKJV)

The Finish Line
In the Bible every book
is set in its place,
To pick up the
momentum
and run that race.

"And let us run with
endurance the race
that is set before us"
(Hebrews 12:1 NKJV).

The Path

Along our walk,
Don't be quick to understand,
Only be willing to hold his hand.

In Him
The Light
L-I-G-H-T
Love In Good Honest Truth

In Him,
none is forgotten,
ALL are remembered by his love.

Life is to be lived,
and not taken for granted.

Everything is so beautiful;
help others see it too.

Within My Heart a Word of Thanks

People have enjoyed what I have done. By
putting smiles on their faces and tears in
they're hearts, I just could not ask for more.
There have been many different expressions, but
overall, they are still the same, happiness and
not sorrows. For I have proved it is not a game. It
is a priceless gift no one could ever pay, so
along with this I would like to say:

In Dedication to My Prayer
I shall follow to as he walks,
And I shall listen to as He talks.
For He will always be in my heart,
And every day shall be a brand-new start.
To the believing in a "Dream."

About the Author

Brett A. Martinez was born and raised in Colorado and enjoys morning and evening walks and taking pictures of the beauty that surrounds him. He enjoys spending his time visiting and volunteering with the elderly at various care facilities in his community and surrounding areas including his local hospital. Overall he enjoys helping others in any way that he can.

CPSIA information can be obtained
at www.ICGtesting.com
Printed in the USA
LVHW070756280721
693888LV00001B/3

9 781638 441373